midwest
west

22

photography 27

contents

PUBLISHER
Alexis Scott

MANAGING EDITOR
Susan Haller

CREATIVE DIRECTOR
Ophelia Chong

ADVERTISING SALES DIRECTOR
Suzanne Semnacher

DIRECTOR OF PRODUCTION
Paul Semnacher

Creative
ART DIRECTOR
Anita Atencio

Advertising Sales
SALES REPRESENTATIVES
Linda Levy
Robert Pastore
Robert Saxon
Lori Watson

ADVERTISING ASSISTANT/NEW YORK
Francesca Meccariello

ADVERTISING ASSISTANT/CHICAGO
Janet Cain

Production
PRODUCTION MANAGER
Jamie Edwards

ON-PRESS PRODUCTION
Lynn D. Pile
Colin Yeung

PRODUCTION
Wendy Walz
Larry Gassan

Book Sales
Mark Williams

Accounting
CHIEF FINANCIAL OFFICER
Jere Clancy

ACCOUNTING ASSISTANT
Eduardo Chevez

FINANCIAL SERVICES
Richard Scott

CHAIRMAN OF THE BOARD
H.B. Scott

VICE-PRESIDENT
Ashley Butler

Workbook 27 Photography Midwest • West
BOOK DESIGN
More Milk Graphic Design

COVER
J. Shubin

END SHEETS
Stephen Chiang

COPY
Paul Gachot

advertisers index

*Artist's Representative

advertisers index

*Artist's Representative

advertisers index

*Artist's Representative

photography east - south pages 1 - 588 | photography midwest - west pages 589 - 1176

advertisers index

*Artist's Representative

advertisers index

*Artist's Representative

advertisers index

*Artist's Representative

midwest west

SANDRO

**MARKUS
GIOLAS**

PHOTOGRAPHER

\+

REPRESENTED BY FORTUNI / 414.964.8088

TOM MADAY 773.235.1600 | www.madayphoto.com

603

CROFOOT
-photography-
tel 612 - 339 - 9191   www.crofootphoto.com

SCIORTINO

Jeff Sciortino Photography
764 N. Milwaukee
Chicago, IL 60622
312.829.6112
www.jeffsciortino.com

Represented by: Jodie Zeitler
312.467.9220
www.jodiezeitler.com

SCIORTINO

Jeff Sciortino Photography
764 N. Milwaukee
Chicago, IL 60622
312.829.6112
www.jeffsciortino.com

Represented by: Jodie Zeitler
312.467.9220
www.jodiezeitler.com

TED TAMBURO PHOTOGRAPHY
3 1 2 . 2 2 6 . 4 8 8 4   www.tamburo-photography.com

represented by Jodie Zeitler   3 1 2 . 4 6 7 . 9 2 2 0

jim *purdum* photography
studio 323.810.8602

midwest jodie zeitler 312.467.9220 east/west nadine kalmes 310.587.2303

michael lande photography & digital imaging

e-LIGHT STUDIOS 219 NORTH JUSTINE STREET CHICAGO IL 60607

T 312.733.1845 F 312.733.3360 www.e-light.com

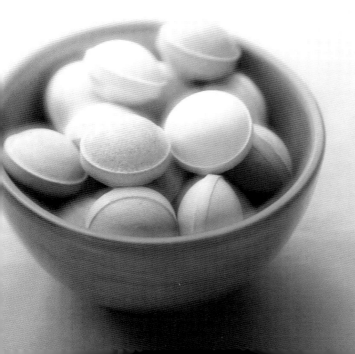

CHRIS DEFORD
PHOTOGRAPHER
1148 West Ohio Chicago, IL 60622 tel 312.666.17

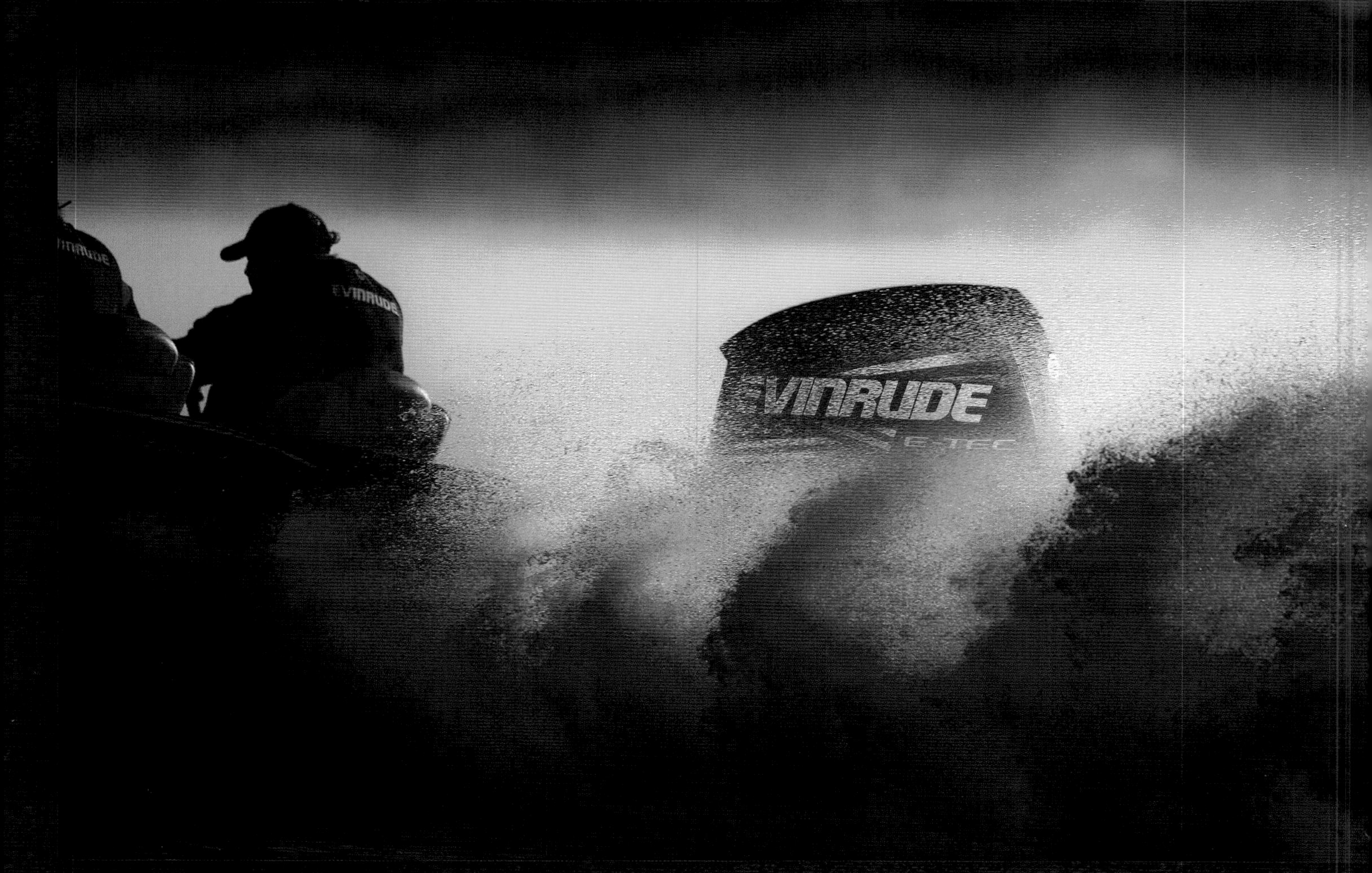

Jim Gallop www.gallop.cor

paul elledge

Paul Elledge   312 397 9888 hq
312 733 8021 tel   212 989 8880 ny   represented by virtū
312 733 3547 fax   415 898 9888 sf   Liz Baugher
paulelledge.com   www.virtu.ws   Candace Gelman

virtū

dave jordano

Dave Jordano   312 397 9888 hq
312 225 0600 tel   212 989 8880 ny   represented by virtù
312 225 7001 fax   415 898 9888 sf   Liz Baugher
jordanophoto.com   www.virtu.ws   Candace Gelman

VIRTU

DARRYLL **SCHIFF**

jeff johnson 612.339.7929

jeffjohnsonphoto.com

represented by robin ogden
612.925.4174

Earl Kendall

612-321-0575

www.kendallphotographs.com

REPRESENTED BY ROBIN OGDEN 612-925-4174

WESTERMAN

CHICAGO (312) 664-5837 • NEW YORK (212) 353-1235
charliewesterman.com

See additional Westerman spread in East/South edition.

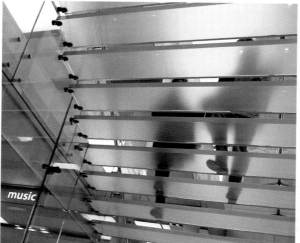

TIM TURNER
STUDIO

steve **becker** photography 95   beckermedia.com   p. 312.286.5533

STIDWILL

STEVE·**PETRO**VICH

SCOTT LANE *road views*

ROBERT NEUMANN

The American Fabric

616 454.1001 | www.bigeventstudios.com

SUSAN KINAST

1504 North Fremont Street

Chicago, Illinois 60622

p. 312-944-6330

f. 312-944-2857

www.kinast.com

kennyjohnson   816.471.1200   www.kennyj.com

Peer Brecht

Peer Brecht

Howard Bjornson

Howard Bjornson - Studio
Tel 312.243.8200
www.howardbjornson.com

Represented by Linda Thomsen
Tel 312.832.1155 Fax 312.832.1156
www.lindathomsen.com

Andy Goodwin

Andy Goodwin - Studio
Tel 312.415.8822
www.agoodwinphoto.com

Represented by Linda Thomsen
Tel 312.832.1155 Fax 312.832.1156
www.lindathomsen.com

Thomsen
GROUP

NOZICKA
877·400·6700

STEVE NOZICKA PHOTOGRAPHY LTD.   CHICAGO, ILLINOIS

HILLARY AIGES
represents
"The Best Art Under The Umbrella"

David
Joseph

Erik
Rank

Tony
Pettinato

www.hillaryaiges.com 212 247 2992

HILLARY AIGES
represents

"The Best Art Under The Umbrella"

Chis
Stanford

Charity

Massimiliano
Cherchi

663

612.827.6719
rmurphy@fishnet.com

PER BREIEHAGEN
P H O T O G R A P H Y

BOB MᶜNAMARA
photography

PAUL NELSON PHOTOGRAPHY   3338 University Ave. SE, Suite 370   Minneapolis, MN 55414   612.623.7696   paulnelsonphoto.com

SAVERIO TRUGLIA

773.278.7584
saveriotruglia.com

NORTHRUP PHOTOGRAPHY

Andrew Northrup 312.455.8155 www.northrup-photography.com represented by Tom Maloney 312.704.0500

NORTHRUP NP PHOTOGRAPHY

Andrew Northrup 312.455.8155   www.northrup-photography.com   represented by Tom Maloney 312.704.0500

VIT O

VITO PALMISANO
PALMISANO PHOTO LTD.

computer generated imagery

tatjana ALVEGAARD

Tatjana Alvegaard Photographie
Studio: 913.219.4645
www.alvegaard.com

photo **KS** kevinsmith

Agent: Anne Albrecht
312 595-0300

www.photokevinsmith.com

photo KS kevinsmith

Agent: Anne Albrecht
312 595-0300

www.photokevinsmith.com

mark katzman

FK

Ferguson & Katzman Photography

ferguson & katzman photography
314.241.3811

mark katzman

assignment: fkphoto.com
stock: haloimages.com

scott ferguson

ferguson & katzman photography
314.241.3811

scott ferguson

assignment: fkphoto.com
stock: haloimages.com

jay baker

Ferguson & Katzman Photography

FK

ferguson & katzman photography
314.241.3811

jay baker

assignment: fkphoto.co
stock: haloimages.co

Matt Marcinkowski

halo images *rights-managed photography*

Matt Marcinkowski

stock: haloimages.com
assignment: fkphoto.com

VEDROS & Associates Photography
vedros.com

VEDROS

Photography and Digital Imaging
more images and stock at vedros.com

Studio | Cathy Kudelko **816 471 5488**
East | Robert Mead Associates **800 717 1994** | RMEADIMAGE.COM

703

SEE OUR 27 PAGES IN THE EAST SECTION.

MITCH MAGNUSON
ST. LOUIS

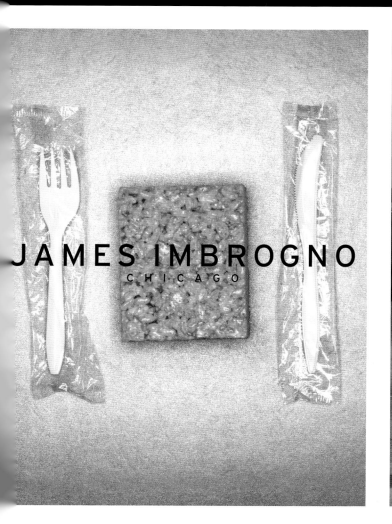
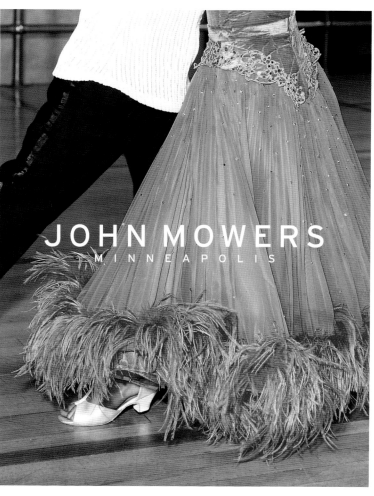

 licious

DARRELL EAGER
612-333-8732

pattisugano&associates

dione white

josh dreyfus

jeff grunewald illustrator

artists representative

pattisugano@aol.com

773.271.4647

www.pattisugano.com

stephen moskop

t. j. hine

akin

deborah fletcher

dionewhite

www.dionewhite.com
represented by pattisugano&associates
pattisugano@aol.com 773.271.4647

T. J. Hine Photography
312.829.7107

represented by pattisugano&associates

DEBORAH FLETCHER
PHOTOGRAPHY, INC.

400 N. Racine #107
Chicago, IL 60622
312.421.2530
heydeb@dfletcherphoto.com
www.dfletcherphoto.com

Represented by
pattisugano&associates
773.271.4647

DEBORAH
FLETCHER
PHOTOGRAPHY, INC.

400 N. Racine #107
Chicago, IL 60622
312.421.2530
heydeb@dfletcherphoto.com
www.dfletcherphoto.com

Represented by
pattisugano&associates
773.271.4647

stephenmoskop

www.stephenmoskop.com
represented by pattisugano&associates
pattisugano@aol.com 773.271.4647

BRUTON | STROUBE

TEL 314 | 241 | 6665

FAX 314 | 241 | 1642

Eat. Shoot. Be Happy.

STEPHEN KENNEDY PHOTOGRAPHY
ST. LOUIS, MISSOURI. 314 621-6545

Location: DESTIN, FLORIDA

Subject: HIGH TIDE

5- 3814

| 1 | 2 | 3 | 4 | 5 | 6 | 7 | 8 | 9 | 10 | 11 | 12 | AM | P | 1 |

STEPHEN KENNEDY PHOTOGRAPHY
ST. LOUIS, MISSOURI. 314 621-6545

Location: SAN RAFAEL, CALIFORNIA

Subject: HIGH SCHOOL REF

5-6114

| 1 | 2 | 3 | 4 | 5 | 6 | 7 | 8 | 9 | 10 | 11 | 12 | AM | P |

karen melvin photography

612.379.7925

karenmelvinphoto.com

karen melvin photography

612.379.7925

karenmelvinphoto.com

slivinski photography

represented by   holly hahn + company

office (312) 633-0500
fax (312) 633-0484
holly@hollyhahn.com

dave slivinski   studio (312) 733-8008
dave@slivinskiphoto.com

Photographer

GREG WHITAKER (812) 988-8808 www.gregwhitaker.com

Represented by Holly Hahn [H²+Co.] (312) 633-0500 holly@hollyhahn.com

www.hollyhahn.com

Photographer

GREG WHITAKER (812) 988-8808 www.gregwhitaker.com

Represented by Holly Hahn [H²+Co.] (312) 633-0500 holly@hollyhahn.com

www.hollyhahn.com

Photographer

dan goldberg

www.goldbergphotography.com
773.484.0577

represented by [H²+Co.]
holly hahn
312.633.0500
www.hollyhahn.com

dan goldberg

mcarthur photography

john and andree mcarthur
studio (312) 666-1212

represented by
holly hahn + company
office (312) 633-0500

mcarthur photography

john and andree mcarthur

studio (312) 666-1212
fax (312) 666-1275
jam@mcarthurphotography.com

represented by

holly hahn + company

office (312) 633-0500
fax (312) 633-0484
holly@hollyhahn.com

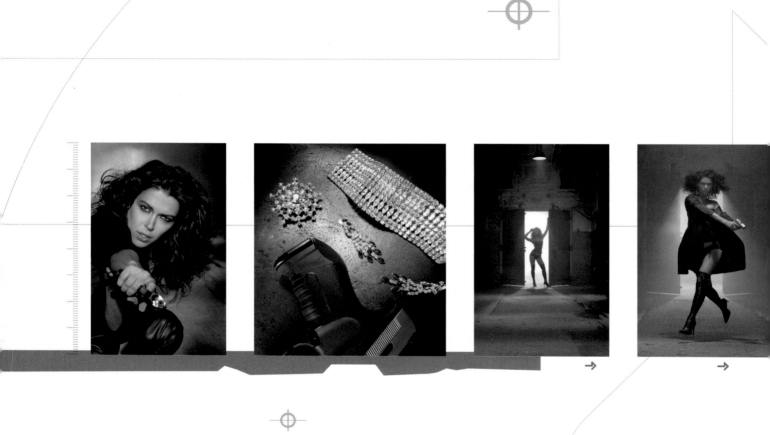

www.**carlohindian**.com

carlo hindian photography

OMAN

RODNEY OMAN BRADLEY
TELEPHONE: 773.395.9211
FACSIMILE: 773.395.2440
WWW.OMAN-E7.COM

David_Radler

Parents Magazine

Cialis/Eli Lilly

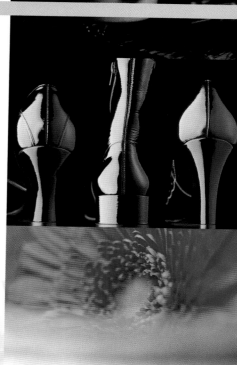

314 960 6303

michael jacob photography

girard

Tod Martens Photography

Studio: 317.639.9610 www.todmartens.com
Represented by Melissa Hennessy: 312.330.0336 www.hennessyreps.com

Tod Martens Photography

Studio: 317.639.9610   www.todmartens.com
Represented by Melissa Hennessy: 312.330.0336   www.hennessyreps.com

S C H U M A N N & C O M P A N Y

PHOTOGRAPHY

Stephen Hamilton

Eric Klein

Alan Shortall

Terry Vine

ILLUSTRATION

Michael Austin

Chris Lockwood

Jing Jing Tsong

Brian White

DESIGN

David Kampa

800.710.1969

www.schumannco.com

Terry Vine Photography

terryvine.com   713 528 6788

Represented by Schumann & Company 800 710 1969

Alan Shortall Photography | 773.252.3747 | www.alanshortall.com

Represented by Schumann & Company | 800.710.1969 | *www.schumannco.com*

STEPHEN HAMILTON PHOTOGRAPHICS

studio: 312.733.4583 | www.stephenhamilton.com

represented by
Schumann & Company
800.710.1969
www.schumannco.com

ERIC KLEIN

ERIC KLEIN

studio 773.227.2122 www.klein-productions.com
represented by Schumann & Company 800.710.1969 www.schumannco.com

STEP 1:

Plan carefully. Not everything comes out in the wash and color mix-ups
tie everyone's underwear in a knot. A delicate problem.
But what happens when the unmentionable becomes obvious?

NIMROD?
IT'S IDIOTPROOF

STEP 2:

When Step 1 puts you on the spot, call Nimrod for expert image assembly and retouching.
Nimrod Systems, Image Alchemists 312.661.0101 www.nimrodsys.com
Represented by Schumann & Company 800.710.1969 www.schumannco.com

JKP

EMBRACE
THE CONCEPT
NAIL THE
CASTING
GET THE SHOT
GET IT AGAIN
SIDEWAYS
EXHALE

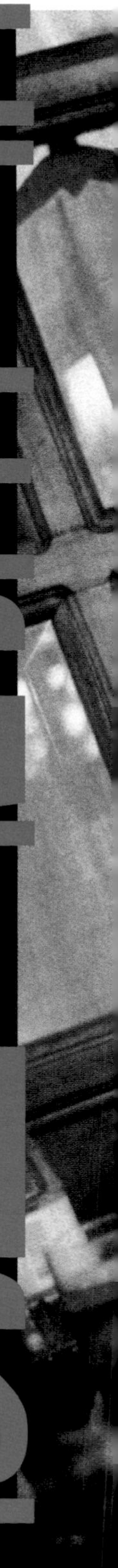

p : 6 1 2 . 2 0 4 . 9 0 1 0
www.sadowskiphoto.com

LAURIE RUBIN

LAURIE RUBIN
Button Represents 312.399.2522
Laura Lemkowitz/New York 212.840.0369
studio: 773.348.2224   www.laurierubin.com

scott payne

www.scottpayne.com ● studio 312.751.9630 ● fax 312.751.9631

represented by Lisa Button ● 312.399.2522 ● www.buttonrepresents.com

www.kuhlphoto.com

kuhlmann
studio

brian warling
represented by
Lisa Button
312 • 399 • 2522

PHOTO 光 GRAHAM

Graham Brown Photography | photograham.com
represented by Fortuni 414-964-8088

PHOTO 光 GRAHAM

Graham Brown Photography | photograham.com
represented by Fortuni 414-964-8088

DON GETSUG STUDIOS • CHICAGO • 312-939-1477 • 312-939-2965/FA

David Lindsey Wade

Represented by Karen Elsesser

262.241.5899 / 262.241.5243 fax / kereps@wi.rr.com

Anyone. Anywhere.

johnnienhuis.com

NĪENHUĪS

CAROLYN SOMLO TALENT

TYLLIE BARBOSA

STEVE GRUBMAN

JIM LUNING

ANDREA MANDEL

456 NORTH MORGAN CHICAGO, ILLINOIS 60622 312-421-2229

grubman.

Steve Grubman Photography, Inc.
456 North Morgan Chicago, IL 60622
312 226-2272
www.grubman.com
Represented by
Carolyn Somlo Talent 312 421-2229
Laura Lemkowitz 212 840-0369
Stock available

andrea mandel   *Represented by* Carolyn Somlo Talent 312.421.2229

andrea mandel

Kevin Banna   www.kevinbanna.c

epresented by Midwest Erica Chadwick T. 773 856 0614 • East/West Marsha Pinkstaff T. 212 799 1500

gregg goldman photography 314.771.7227
www.goldmanphoto.com

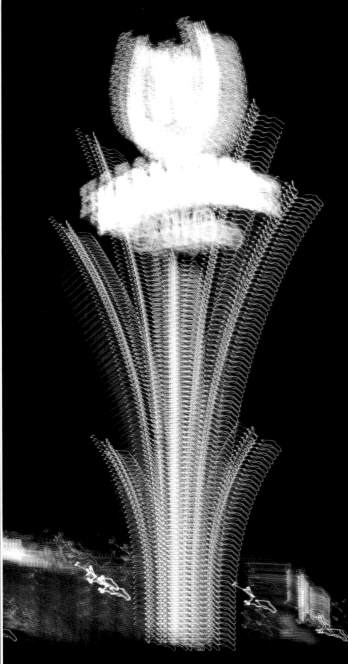

Scott Ritenour

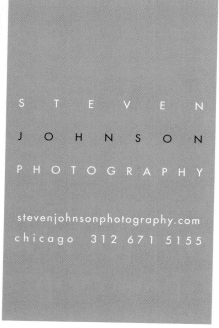

LIVE LIKE YOU MEAN IT

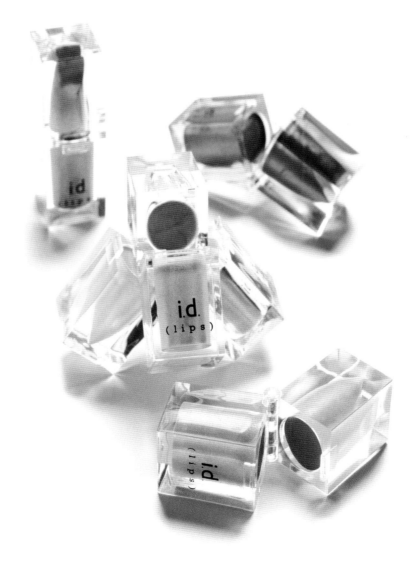

STEVE EWERT PHOTOGRAPHY   ewertphoto.com   312.733.5762

JOHN WELZENBACH PRODUCTIONS
847.640.7878   f 847.640.7886

JOHN WATSON

EYEFIRE

eric hausman

P 312 243 7811 **F** 312 243 7822

312 N. MAY STREET, SUITE 2K, CHICAGO, IL 60607

INFO@SHAPPSPHOTOGRAPHY.COM

SHAPPS PHOTOGRAPHY

REPRESENTED BY BOB WOLTER — 312 715 0100

WWW.SHAPPSPHOTOGRAPHY.COM

John McCallum | REPRESENTED BY WANDA 312.733.0800

John McCallum | Represented by Wanda 312.733.0800

help

840

ShaneMorgan

312.226.2292
shanemorgan.com

Represented by
Patrice Bockos
312.661.1777

ShaneMorgan

312.226.2292
shanemorgan.com

Represented by
Patrice Bockos
312.661.1777

greg heck

photography

ph 312.226.2660

fax 312.226.2777

www.heckphoto.com

represented by

Bockos Creative Representation

ph 312.661.1777

fax 312.661.1745

CHARLIE SIMOKAITIS
REPRESENTED BY BOCKOS CREATIVE
PHONE: 312.661.1777
WWW.SIMOKAITISPHOTOGRAPHY.COM

CHARLIE SIMOKAITIS

REPRESENTED BY BOCKOS CREATIVE
PHONE: 312.661.1777
WWW.SIMOKAITISPHOTOGRAPHY.COM

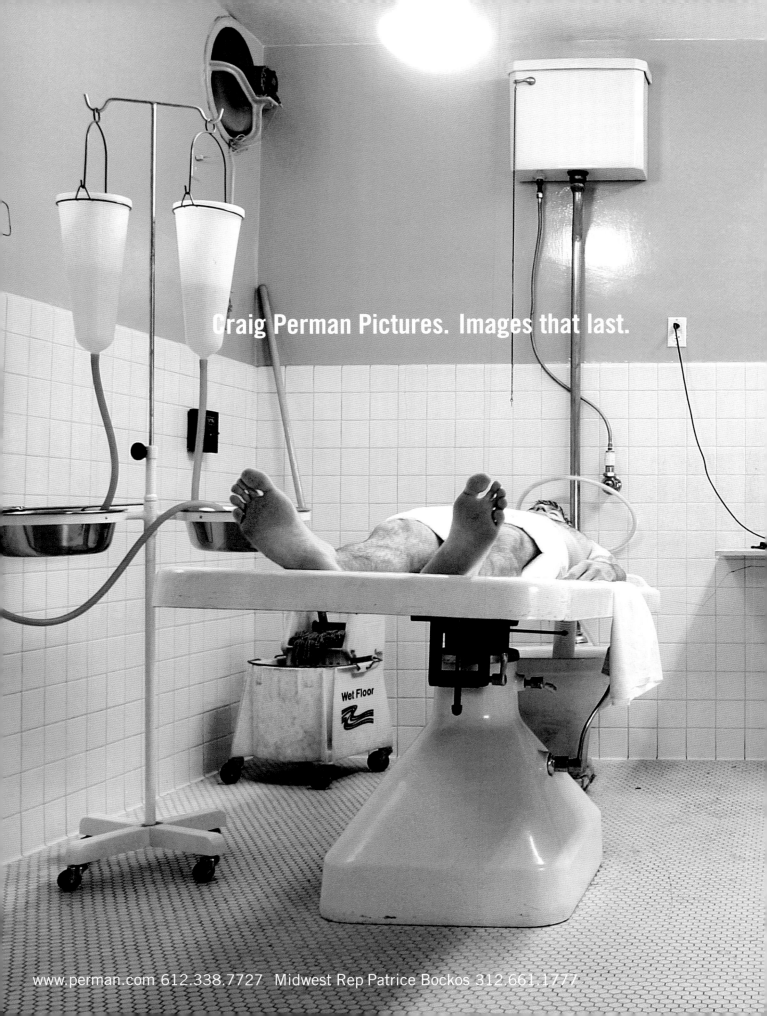

Craig Perman Pictures. Images that last.

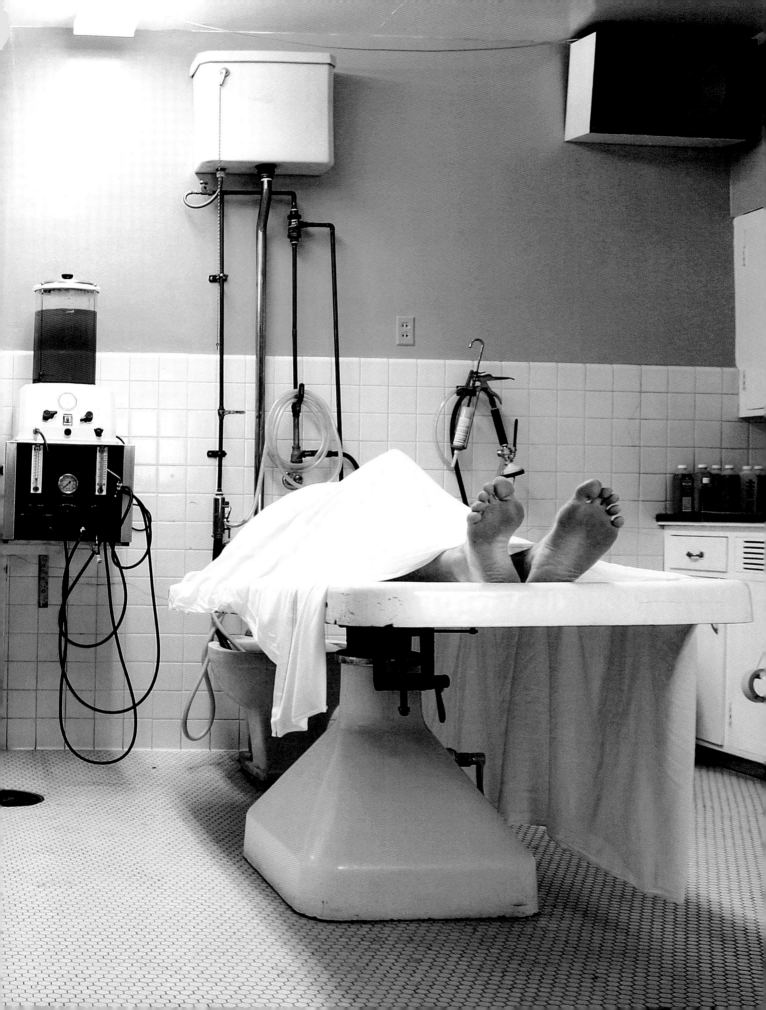

Part 3: The Beginning of the Split Ends...

As civilizations grew and tribes formed across the globe, hair began taking on local character. Where the Egyptians cherished a complex waterfall-coif of fine braids and beads, the Jamaicans wore mighty dreadlocks pressed with fresh herbs and tannins. But of all the diverse hair stylings on Earth, two memorably coifed tribes in particular shared a most profound, and yet largely unspoken, power struggle of hair-raising proportions. Interestingly, like most struggles rooted in a polarity, this one was born of a deep need for the two wildly different tribes to co-exist. The Creats (known for their fancy-colored plumes and alternating shaved areas of the scalp) and the Adbyres (recognizable for their tasteful, salon-manufactured dos) were forever destined to work in tandem, bringing new and exciting messages of new and improved products to all the hair-loving tribes of our fair planet.

Read Parts 3 & 4 in *Workbook Midwest Photography West* and Parts 5 & 6 in *Workbook Illustration*
or at www.workbook.com/sixparts.html

The cyclical struggles over creative control in the realms of the ad world quagmire as told through the story of hair (in 6 parts)

by Paul Gachot

midwest west

The cyclical struggles over creative control in the realms of the ad world quagmire as told through the story of hair (in 6 parts)

by Paul Gachot

midwest

west

Part 4: Crew Cuts and Color Damage.

But who would lead and who would follow? This was the eternal question that propelled decades of tumultuous rumblings among the Creats and the Adbyres. Initially, the Adbyres with their superior organizational and book-keeping skills (not to mention their neat professional hair) were able to keep the wild impulses of the Creats well submerged. And while the messages they built together were often less than inspiring, together they did slowly grow into a mighty empire which much gold and power were invested. Throughout this era the Creats begged for more of a say in how the messages they produced were presented, but for the time being the Adbyres said, "Trust us! We know better." But as the decades progressed, it wasn't just the Creats who were yearning for more. The world was growing tired of bland messaging and neat hair. New legions of shaggy rebellious youth from tribes all over would clamor for something different.

Read Parts 3 & 4 in *Workbook Midwest Photography West* and Parts 5 & 6 in *Workbook Illustration* or at www.workbook.com/sixparts.html

cash

ron ESHEL

Rhoni Epstein Associates

west 310.207.5937
east 917.597.7211

sally bjornsen represents

kathryn barnard

henry blackham

david clugston

alex hayden

zee wendell

www.sallyreps.com | 1 866 857 0063

kathryn barnard | www.sallyreps.com

henry blackham | www.sallyreps.com

david clugston | www.sallyreps.com

alex hayden | www.sallyreps.com

www.**philipsalaverryphoto**.com 415.252.8090

STEVEN LIPPMAN 818 880 1170   www.stevenlippman.com

www.shutokonami.com
studio: 323.828.6598

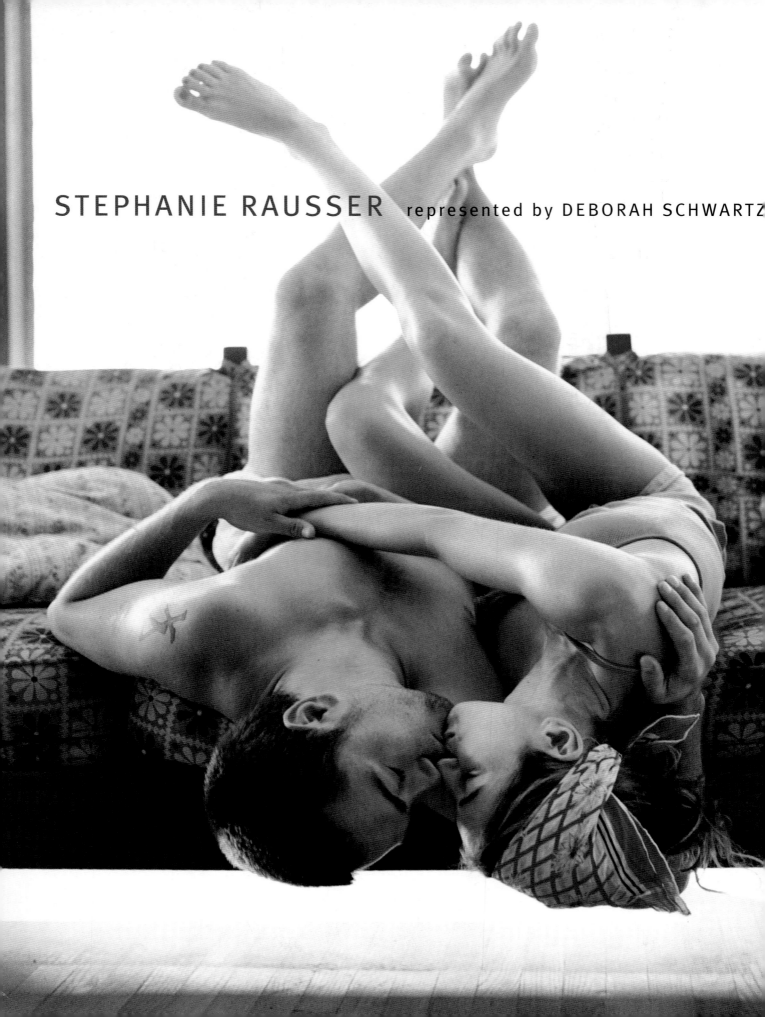

STEPHANIE RAUSSER represented by DEBORAH SCHWARTZ

"Lettuce is like conversation: It must be fresh and crisp, and so sparkling that you scarcely notice the bitter in it."

C.D. Warner, 19th century

james CARRIER

415.777.1266

Douglas Adesko Photography tel. (415) 648-3800

Rep EAST John Kenney & tel. (914) 962-0002

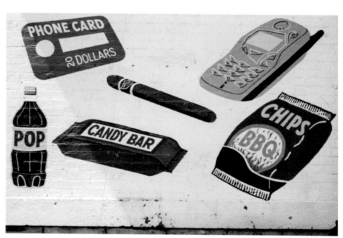

Rep WEST Freda Scott tel. (415) 550-9121

STUART SCHWARTZ

stuartschwartz.com

san francisco
415.388.1760

rep freda scott
415.550.9121

Christopher Irion

415.643.8986
irionphotography.com

Christopher Irion
415.643.8986
irionphotography.com

West Coast
representation by
Freda Scott, Inc.
415.550.9121
fredascott.com

Midwest
representation by
Tom Maloney
312.704.0500
tommaloneyreps.com

MARSHALL GORDON

PHOTOGRAPHY 415.552.9832 **STUDIO**

REPRESENTED BY FREDA SCOTT 415.550.9121

C OBLEIGH

M A T T   C O B L E I G H
AT JOECARLSONSTUDIO   626.799.3430
KATHEE TOYAMA REPRESENTS   626.791.9301
                                     www.mattcobleigh.com

Self-Promotion

1 (series)
  Tim Mantoani, photographer
  Personal Project, "Havana is Calling"

2 Tim Mantoani, photographer
  Directv, client
  Juan Dixon

3 Tim Mantoani, photographer
  NHL - Center Ice, client
  Olaf Kolzig

Frank Meo, Representative,
  212 643 7428
Studio, 800 543 9960
www.mantoani.com, web

G L E N N ❧ O A K L E Y

GLENN ❧ OAKLEY

oakleyphoto.com   glenn@oakleyphoto.com   208.383.9163

Lifestyle

Joel Grimes Photography

the
interpretation
project

Now representing: Andy Anderson, Ann Cutting,
David Bowman, David Martinez, Hunter Freeman,
Noel Barnhurst, and Thomas Broening

Please contact Heather Elder or
Lauranne Lospalluto at:

415.285.7709 Tel
415.285.7979 Fax
office@heatherelder.com

1037 Church Street
San Francisco, CA 94114
www.heatherelder.com

heather elder

David Bowman Photography
4720 South Lyndale Avenue
Minneapolis, MN 55419

612 209 0844 Tel
david@bowmanstudio.com
www.bowmanstudio.com

Represented by Heather Elder
415 285 7709 Tel
www.heatherelder.com

david bowman

BOBS

As Graydon prepared for this shoot, he told me how the park had spoken to him over the years, giving him advice. I asked what kind of advice he'd sought, and he said it was always the same. Thirty years ago, he gave up a writing career and sold insurance to support his family. Said he'd only written one line of verse since then, on this very bench. After the shoot, I asked him if the park had spoken today. He smiled and said "Oh, yes. The answer has never changed." He shook my hand, I thanked him for his time and he left. As I gathered my things, I saw these words carved in the bench where he'd sat: "Don't Eat Your Soul To Feed Your Belly..."

andy

ANDY ANDERSON phone: 208.587.3161 fax: 208.587.6139 url: www.andyandersonphoto.com
Represented by Heather Elder phone: 415.285.7709 fax: 415.285.7979

Noel Barnhurst
NoelBarnhurst.com

Ann e. Cutting 626_440_1974 www.cutting.com   represented by heather elder 415_285_7709 www.heatherelder.com

Ann e. Cutting 626_440_1974 www.cutting.com represented by heather elder 415_285_7709 www.heatherelder.com

917

152 Mississippi Street
San Francisco, CA 94107
415 252 1910 phone
415 252 1917 fax
hunterfreeman.com

Represented by
Heather Elder
415 285 7709 phone
415 285 7979 fax
heatherelder.com

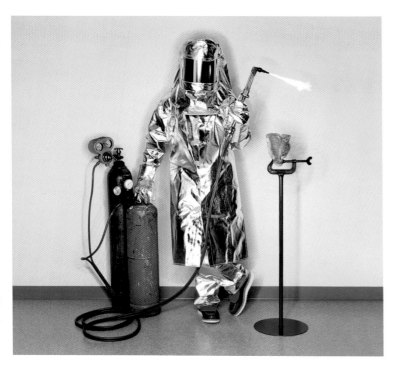

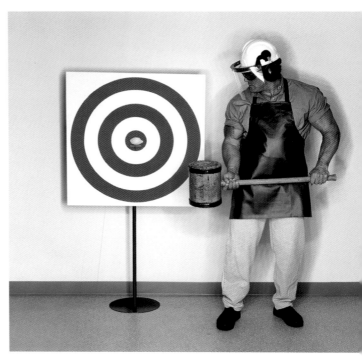

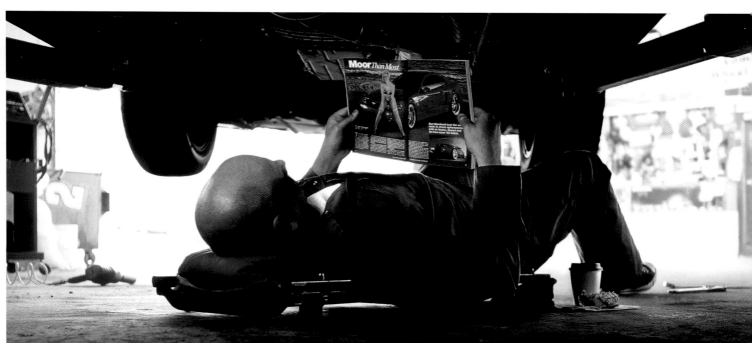

152 Mississippi Street
San Francisco, CA 94107
415 252 1910 phone
415 252 1917 fax
hunterfreeman.com

Represented by
Heather Elder
415 285 7709 phone
415 285 7979 fax
heatherelder.com

DAVID MARTINEZ

DAVID MARTINEZ STUDIO   415.543.7008   davidmartinezstudio.com

represented by heather elder   415.285.7709   heatherelder.com

WAHLBERG

SAN FRANCISCO

www.chriswahlberg.com   415.821.6906

Michael Leland

Jay & Ani

Tamara Muth-King

Lisa Loftus

emy Goldberg

Mark Scoggins

n Leuner

06 Lawler St Los Angeles CA 90066
0 390 0763 f 310 390 2918
Broadway #706 New York NY 10010
2 465 3244
is@artistsmgmt.com
ica@artistsmgmt.com
w.artistsmgmt.com

ARTISTS MANAGEMENT, INC.

DANI WINSTON
888.751.3341 | INFO@WINSTONSTUDIOS.COM | WWW.WINSTONSTUDIOS.COM

WINSTON
STUDIOS

95180

hamilton gray
& associates

hamiltongray.com

P 213 380 3933
F 213 380 2906

E info@hamiltongray.com

photographers : matthew barnes / jay blakesberg / john clark / vern evans

michael grecco / sandra johnson / george lange / michael llewellyn

vivica menegaz / roxann arwen mills / joseph rafferty / shelly strazis

john clark 503.239.4639 represented by hamilton gray & associates 213.380.3933 hamiltongray.com

Sutter Home

Target

Serta

Sony

Red Envelope

Semiliquid

sandra johnson ⤜ photography ⤛ **323 462 6888**

MATTHEW BARNES
STUDIO 323 257 0629
www.matthewbarnesphotography.com

Represented by
HAMILTON GRAY & ASSOCIATES
213 380 3933
info@hamiltongray.com
www.hamiltongray.com

MATTHEW BARNES

STUDIO 323 257 0629
www.matthewbarnesphotography.com

Represented by
HAMILTON GRAY & ASSOCIATES
213 380 3933
info@hamiltongray.com
www.hamiltongray.com

shellystrazis.com 562 930 0095 represented by hamilton gray 213 380 3933

shelly strazis PHOTOGRAPHY

shellystrazis.com   562 930 0095   represented by hamilton gray 213 380 3933

ERN EVANS PHOTOGRAPHY

represented by
Hamilton Gray & Associates
www.hamiltongray.com

323.227.1270 studio
213.380.3933 HG&A
www.vernevansphoto.com

MICHAEL LLEWELLYN
STUDIO (323) 223-1792
www.michaelllewellyn.com
Represented by HAMILTON GRAY & ASSOCIATES
(213) 380-3933   www.hamiltongray.com

Jay Blakesberg Photography

Represented by Hamilton Gray 213-380-3933

WWW.BLAKESBERG.COM   JAY@BLAKESBERG.COM   STUDIO 415-621-2366

Jay Blakesberg Photography

HEATHER MONAHAN PHOTOGRAPHY

BRAD COHEN PHOTOGRAPHY
213 924 1745

BRAD COHEN PHOTOGRAPHY
213 924 1745

SEE OUR 27 PAGES IN THE EAST SECTION.

RICHARD WAHLSTROM
SAN FRANCISCO

séamus photography

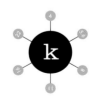

Lisa Keenan Photography

Emeryville California
voice: 510 547 8222   fax: 510 547 8221

www.lisakeenan.com

I view the world a little differently.

STEVEN *Moeder*

DAVE *Lauridson*

DANIEL *Hennessy*

JOAO *Canziani*

STEVE *Simko*

MICHAEL *Weschler*

JACK *Thompson*

michael weschler photography

957

DAVE LAURIDSEN   REPRESENTED BY **LEAH LEVINE**   **818 783 7241**

Jack Thompson

people | places

L² Agency
Leah Levine
818.783.7241
LA | Houston

DANIEL HENNESSY PHOTOGRAPHY   DANIELHENNESSYPHOTOGRAPHY.COM

MOEDER

Los Angeles / San Francisco

JOÃO CANZIANI PHOTOGRAPHER
represented by leah levine tel (818) 783 7241 fax (818) 783 7307

joaocanziani.com

MICHAEL SEXTON

SAN FRANCISCO

415.621.5345   WWW.SEXTONARTS.COM

MICHAEL SEXTON

SAN FRANCISCO

415.621.5345   WWW.SEXTONARTS.COM

night and day...

RIC FRAZIER

DAVID HANOVER PHOTOGRAPHY

STUDIO: 323.462.5695

FAX: 323.462.6360

EMAIL: DHANOVER@EARTHLINK.NET

WEB: DAVIDHANOVER.COM

play

Graves

WWW.RICKGRAVES.COM

7 1 4 • 6 6 2 • 2 6 2 3

JOHN MARIAN PHOTOGRAPHY

STUDIO: 310.324.7651   FAX: 310.324.7652   EMAIL: jmarianphoto@sbcglobal.net   WEB: www.jmarianphoto.com

CHUCK KUHN

PHOTOGRAPHER/FILM DIRECTOR SEATTLE (206)842-1996

BRIAN BAILEY

WWW.BRIANBAILEYPHOTOGRAPHY.COM
970-704-9004

MJORDANPHOTOGRAPHY.COM LA 818 880 9149 NY 212 727 2007
REPRESENTED BY WHITE CROSS

glenwexler.com | 323 465.0268

elizabeth pojé represents.....

john konkal

bill cahill

tony garcia

jack andersen

trudi unger

trevor pearson

ron berg

david ash

michael bisco

tim damon - l.a.

eric schmidt

shim

skyra

jim smithson

illustrators:

frank kozik

the pizz

l.a. 310.556.1439

n.y.c. 212.222.2921

"stop living as though you were dying," nick says as blossom leans over the safety bar, rocking the carriage. they've been stalled at the top of the ferris wheel for 45 minutes and blossom decides they need a drink. she opens her straw box purse and hands nick the etched silver flask she always carries, once a gift from their father to her mother. she studies the random geometry of the ground below, the curved asphalt pathways, browned topiary, drifting balloons, and children clustered like sheep on the way to the petting zoo. the

curses and commands of repairmen drift upwards, along with the yapping rant of a woman rotund enough to be mistaken for an orange on stilts. blossom realizes the woman is wearing shorts and she winces, as though she could feel the raw chafe of the woman's inner thighs. the breeze turns chilly and blossom feels nick's warm hand in her lap. she closes her eyes as the wheel lurches forward 10 degrees. "don't stop," she says.....

konkal.com

konkal

...john konkal is represented by elizabeth pojé @ 310.556.1439 or give john a call

0.824.2027. and if the shoe fits, he's in..

...bill cahill is represented by elizabeth pojé @ 310.556.1439 or call bill

bill-cahill.com

cahill

818.363.1297. he deserves the chair, so to speak...

tonygarcia.com

garcia

xt job with tony @ 323.463.8260 and make a big splash...........................

jackandersen.com

andersen

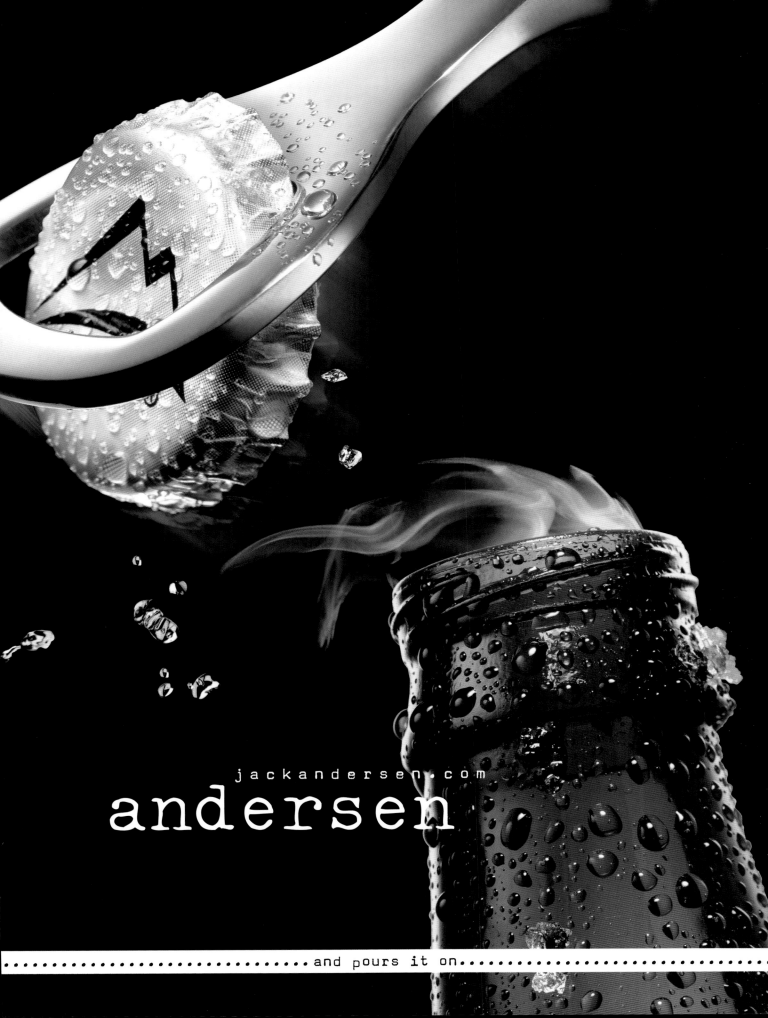

5.381.5683 to capture life's little pleasures..........................

pearson

pearson

..... nobody rides for free...

ronbergphoto.com

berg

816.842.8480. statistics show men think about scoring every three minutes....

www.marcsimonphoto.com   415.864.5606

represented by JENNIFER CHAPMAN 415.505.0545

www.marcymaloy.com

Marshal Safron Studios   tel. 323. 817. 1888   www.safronstudio.com

Viktor Polson

Randy Schwartz

Martin Esseveld

Jon McKee

Paul Goirand

Bonnie Holland

C.J. Burton

Olivier Pojzman

1020

bonnie **h**olland

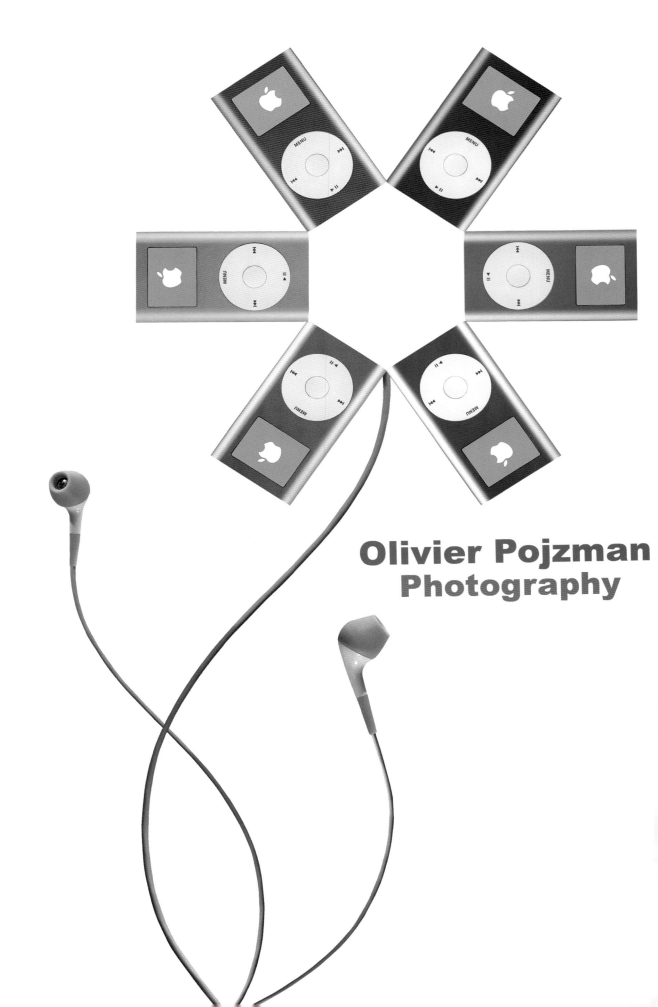

Olivier Pojzman
Photography

www.velvetartists.com   323./82.0992
olivier pojzman

www.**cjburton**.com
studio **403.289.1501**

the new Honey Mustard **Turkey Sub**

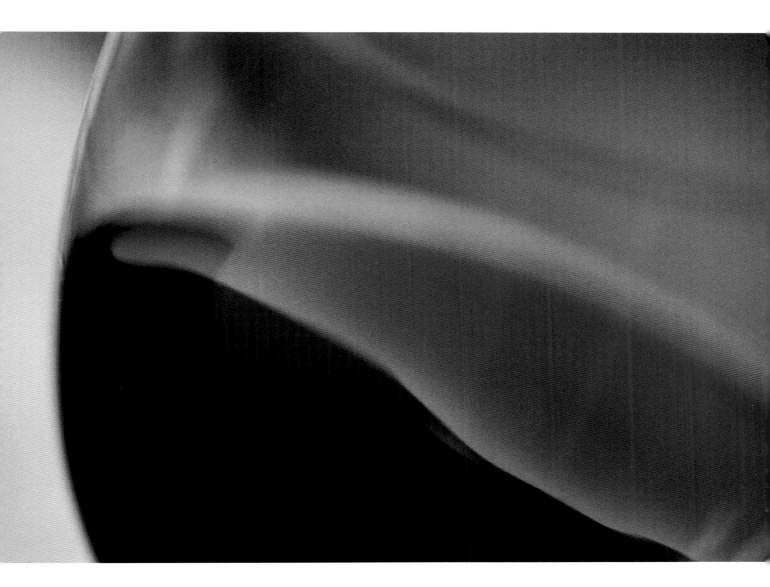

ESKITE
PHOTOGRAPHY

Assignment · Stock · Digital
415.626.9606
www.eskite.com

NOZICKA
877·400·6700

STEVE NOZICKA PHOTOGRAPHY LTD.   CHICAGO, ILLINOIS

LADERA RANCH, CALIFORNIA

Lew Robertson
photography / digital imaging

310.837.7009 www.lewrobertson.com

JAMES SALZANO

Represented by
Marianne Campbell Associates
415.433.0353
mariannecampbell.com

Salzano Studio
212.242.4820
salzanophoto.com

Celine, Miami

L^MOTTE

VENERA

DAVID ZAITZ

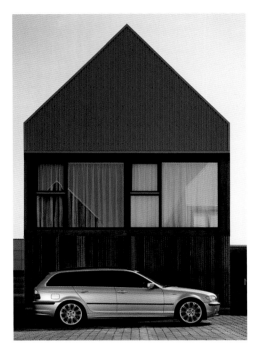

ERIK CHMIL

PETER SAMUELS

DEDDENS+DEDDENS

artist representation

DAVID ZAITZ
ERIK CHMIL
PETER SAMUELS
TOM BURKHART
NICK KOUDIS
JEFF WIGHT
NATALIE BOEHM
ALAN ROSS
CATRINA GENOVESE

310 205 9225
deddensart.com

TOM BURKHART

NICK KOUDIS

JEFF WIGHT

NATALIE BOEHM

Myron Beck Photography
West Coast 323•933•9883
Mid West Rep: Joel Harlib 312•573•1370
East Coast Rep: Greg Sellentin 212•736•0488

∞ People

∞ Animals

∞ Food

∞ Still Life

∞ Western

∞ **Visit: www.myronbeck.com** ∞

LEXUS

KAWASAKI

CHRIS WIMPEY

WWW.CHRISWIMPEY.COM

619.297.3931

HARLEY-DAVIDSON

LEXUS

CHRIS WIMPEY

WWW.CHRISWIMPEY.COM

619.297.3931

jimpurdum.com

jim **purdum** photography
studio 323.810.8602

west/east nadine kalmes 310.587.2303   midwest jodie zeitler 312.467.9220

**Nadine
Kalmes**

artist
rep

(310)

587
2303

Rocki Pedersen Photography

2924 2nd Street . Santa Monica CA 90405 . **O** 310.399.5244 . **F** 310.399.4645 . rockipedersen.com (ROCKI)

steve Bonini Photography
stevebonini.com
503.222.6020

stevebonini.com

Rep. nadine kalmes 310.587.2303

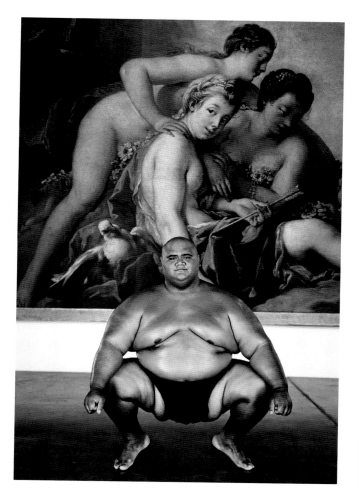

STUDIO 310 823 4228 **FAX** 310 823 5395 **WEB** WWW.MEIGNEUX.COM

PATRICE
MEIGNEUX

Nadine

Kalmes

artist
rep

(310)

587
2303

Nadine

Kalmes

artist
rep

(310)

587

2303

STUDIO
626 568 3252

RICK CHOU STUDIO

Timothy Baur
Photography
www.baurphoto.com

Nadine

Kalmes

artist
rep

(310)

587
2303

s^ja^er^fp^fa

James Caulfield
Animate
Inanimate
[312] 733-8620

Cameron Davidson
Aerial
[703] 845-0547

Walt Denson
People
Location
[415] 331-5555

Tony Garcia
Contemporary
Life style
[323]463-8260

Tatjana Alvegaard
Children
Location
Portraits
[913] 219-4645

Alex Viarnes
Real life
Location
[808] 538-0800

Tim Mantoani
Action
Sports
Celebrities
[619] 543-9959

Suebarr
Family
Children
Lifestyle
[212] 946-5790

Stuart Heir
Product
[212] 633-2187

Ron Berg
Location
Lifestyle
[816] 842-8480

Gordon Watkinson
Sensual
Mood & Texture
[646] 235-5601

Robert Grimm
Food
Product
Beverage
[314] 436-9797

Ric Frazier
Underwater
[310] 559-1441

joSon
Places
Lifestyle
Sports Portraits
[415] 447-6011

Ric Cohn
People
Expressive Products
[212] 924-4450

Michael Back
People
Travel
Lifestyle
[919] 833-0374

George Contorakes
People
Location
[305] 661-0731

Paolo Marchesi
People
Location
Outdoors
[406] 585-0747

Mitchel Gray
Action
Bodies
Sports Celebrities
[212] 665-1481

Keith Berr
Dramatic
Spontaneity
Collaboration
[216] 566-7950

Chris Hamilton

Motion
Advertising
Real Situations

[404] 355-9411

Caterina Bernardi

Nudes
Fashion
portraits

[415] 948-3031

David Alan Wolters

People
Beauty
Fantasy

[616] 844-6909

Cade Martin

People
Travel
Corporate

[202] 986-2805

Suzette Troche-Stapp
a.k.a "the glitterguru"

Glitter
Digital
Beauty

[661] 799-9131

Caesar Lima

People
Unique Still-life

[818] 223-8184

Brad Feinknopf

Interiors
Evocative Architecture

[614] 324-0602

Andy Batt

Creative
Collaborative Visions

[503] 238-9914

Burk Jackson

Clean
Strong
Progressive

[503] 475-9056

Steven Edson

Things
Places
People

[617] 527-2424

Jack Perno

Beauty
Fashion

[312] 666-1495

Alison Barnes Martin

Clean
Happy
Bright

[816] 474-4510

John Sibilski

Life Portraits

[414] 405-4607

David Sacks

Product
Still-Life

[212] 929-9382

Barbara Karant

Interiors
Exteriors
Room-Sets

[312] 733-0891

Mark Robert Halper

People
Digital & Film

[888] 273-2838

Ahop2photography.com

J.W. Fry

Conceptual

[415] 379-9205

Jeff Heger

People
Worldwide
Landscapes

[713] 942-7102

Jensen Hande

Travel
Portrait
Location

[888] 920-0910

AHOP2 · Photography & Illustration

BANK OF AMERICA   CINTAS   WEIGHT WATCHERS   VISA   KING WORLD   MARIE CLAIRE   ANNE COLE SWIMWEAR   CRISTINA FERRARE   HEWLETT PACKARD   CBS

CHARLES WILLIAM BUSH   •   323 466 6630   •   888 646 8006   •   studio@charlesbush.com
CHICAGO, BOB WOLTER   •   312 670 8770   •   bwolter@earthlink.net

DB NEEDHAN   MERCEDES BENZ   MAYBELLINE   NEUTROGENA   CLARION   PARAMOUNT   UNIVERSAL MUSIC   DISNEY   ENTERTAINMENT TONIGHT   TOYOTA

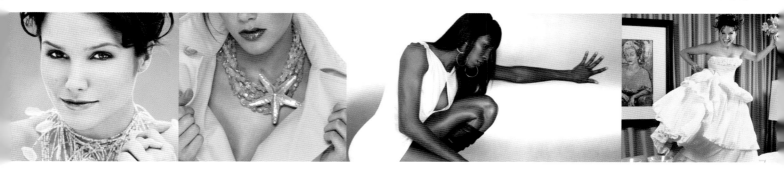

www.charlesbush.com

Ron Krisel Photography
310.477.5519 • www.krisel.com

RICHARD REINSDORF

RICHARD REINSDORF

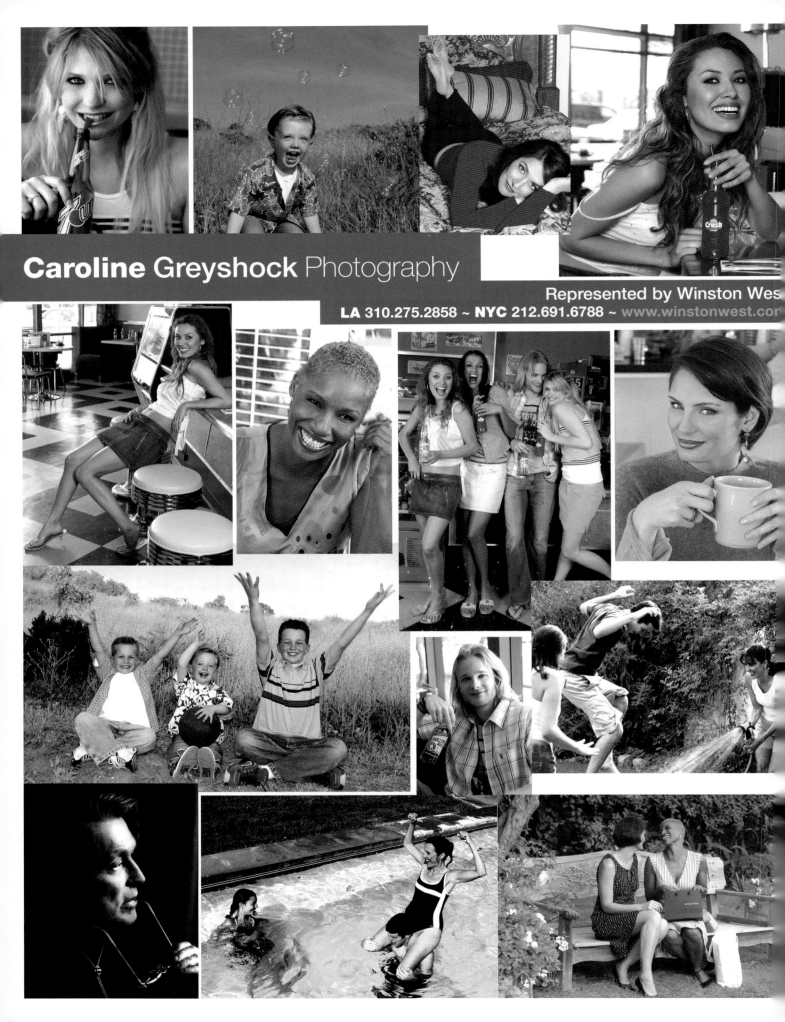

Caroline Greyshock Photography

Represented by Winston West

LA 310.275.2858 ~ NYC 212.691.6788 ~ www.winstonwest.com

LAURA DOSS PHOTOGRAPHY
WWW.LAURADOSS.COM

REPRESENTED BY:
WINSTON WEST
NEW YORK: 212.691.6788
LOS ANGELES: 310.275.285

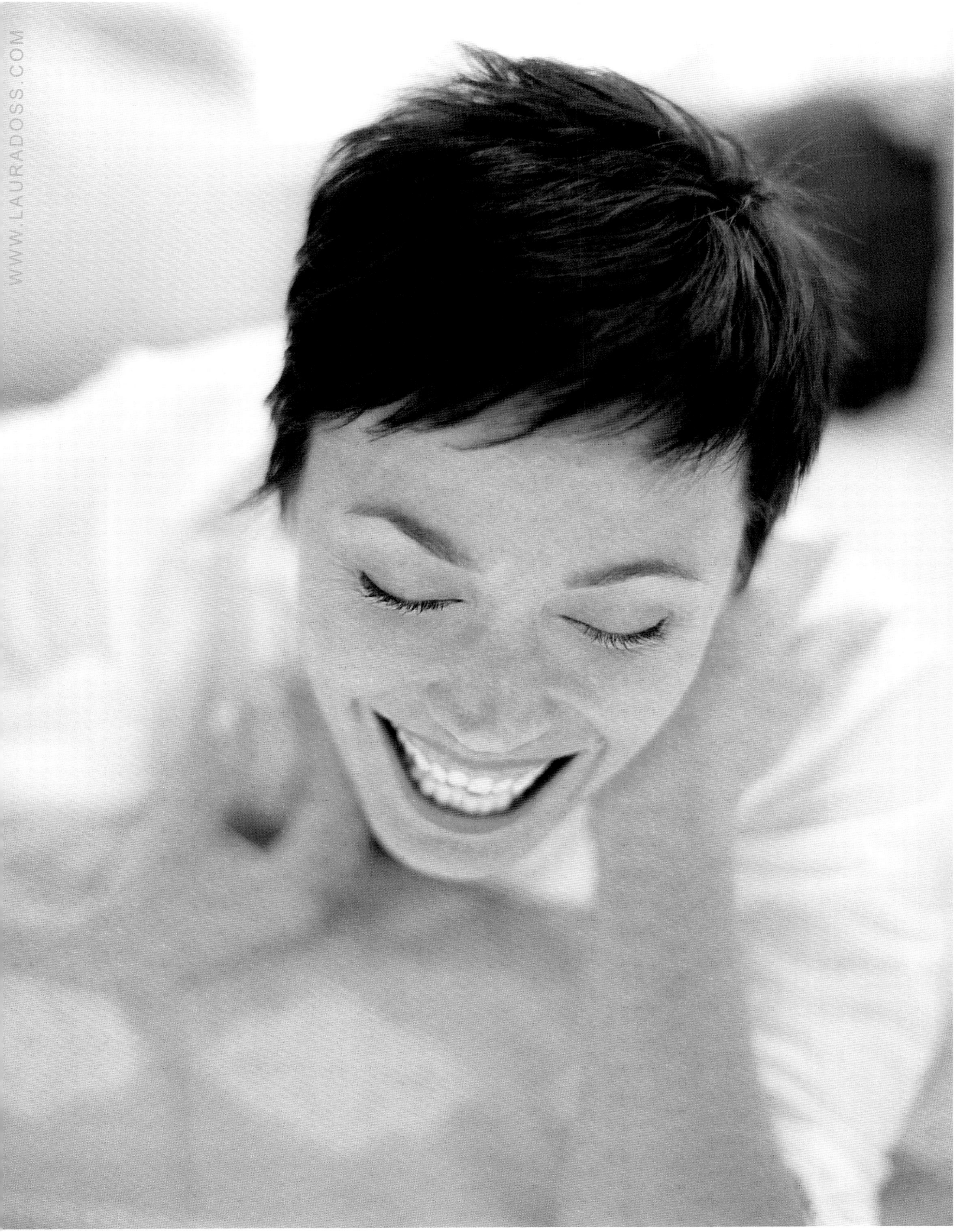

WWW.LAURADOSS.COM

steve hix

studio | hixphoto.com
805.523.7100

midwest | Emily Inman
312.836.6382

new york | Karen Russo
212.749.6382

Fairmont Resort / Chanting to the Water Gods

Hyatt Regency / Observatory Deck

Grand Wailea Resort / Mineral Baths

Ritz Carlton / Half Moon Bay

RICHARD
HUME PHONE 310 827 0450
HUMEPHOTO.COM

KENSAX PHOTOGRAPHY · Represented by Bob Wolter · 312.715.0100 · LA 310.785.0335 · WEB-SITE - WWW.KENSAX.COM

eö

erik östling photography

tel 801 364 3686

toll free 888 383 3686

www.eophoto.com

BYLLWILLIAMS.COM

BYLL WILLIAMS

REPRESENTED BY
LISA ELLISON
323.259.2400

Aaron Geis Photography

(503) 880 8683 studio
represented by Lisa Ellison
(323) 259 2400 phone
(323) 259 2442 fax
aarongeis.com

Aaron Geis Photography

(503) 880 8683 studio
represented by Lisa Ellison
(323) 259 2400 phone
(323) 259 2442 fax
aarongeis.com

DANNEHL

DENNIS DANNEHL STUDIO
DENNIS@DANNEHL.COM
213.388.3888

Michael Voorhees
photographer

Studio 949-650-6150
newport beach, ca

Voorheesphoto.com
haleiwa, hawaii

the O.C.   and it's all good on the North Shore !
Team O'Neill 2005"   keep it real!

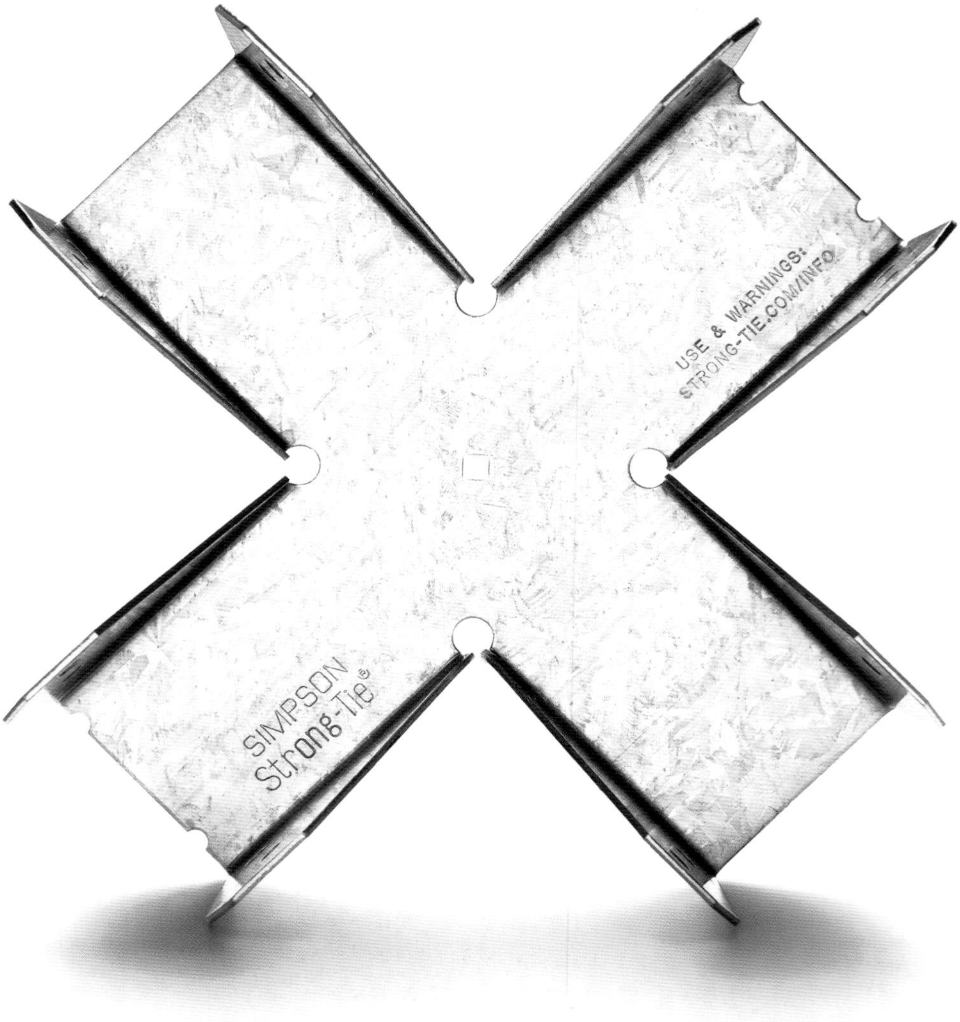
USE & WARNINGS:
STRONG-TIE.COM/INFO
SIMPSON
Strong-Tie®

SWINTEK

rep: andrea stern   310.574.0076

BOY SCOUTS OF AMERICA

Seductively Smooth

Experience the seduction of Black Velvet Canadian Whisky.
Premium. Imported. *Smooth As Velvet.*

BLACK VELVET

Black Velvet® Canadian Whisky, 40% ALC/VOL. (80 Proof). Imported and bottled by the Black Velvet Distilling Company, Chicago, IL.

S I L V E R M A N

1541 N. Cahuenga Blvd. • Hollywood, California 90028
Tel 323-466-6030 • Fax 323-466-7139 • www.jaysilverman.com
Call for our Portfolio or Reel • Contact: Anne Medcalf

Small Business

VISA

Small Business

VISA

Flexible solutions for your success

BUDWEISER

SILVERMAN

1541 N. Cahuenga Blvd. • Hollywood, California 90028
Tel 323-466-6030 • Fax 323-466-7139 • www.jaysilverman.com
Call for our Portfolio or Reel • Contact: Anne Medcalf

MARK McLANE PHOTOGRAPHY

SAN FRANCISCO

WWW.MCLANEPHOTO.COM

STUDIO 415.332.7600

marc addleman

larry bartholomew

dorian caster

robert deutschman

don diaz

tiff pemberton

Alyssa Pizer

310 440 3930
alyssapizer.com

Marc Addleman

PHOTOGRAPHER

ALYSSA PIZER MANAGEMENT   310 440 3930   ALYSSAPIZER.COM

LARRY BARTHOLOMEW

REPRESENTED BY ALYSSA PIZER   310 440 3930   ALYSSAPIZER.COM

DORIAN CASTER

ROBERT DEUTSCHMAN   REPRESENTED BY ALYSSA PIZER   310 440 3930   WWW.ROBERTDEUTSCHMAN.COM

REPRESENTED BY ALYSSA PIZER

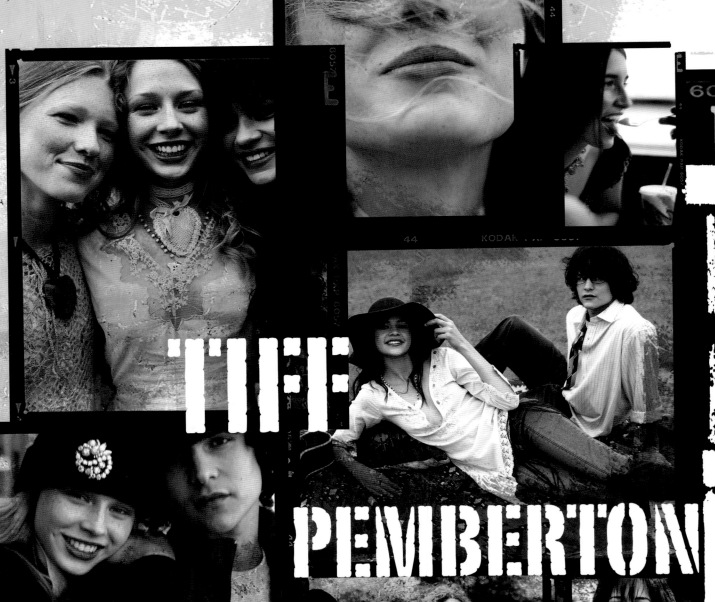

TIFF
PEMBERTON

44   KODAK PXP 6057

6 1 9

2 8 0

9 9 0 0

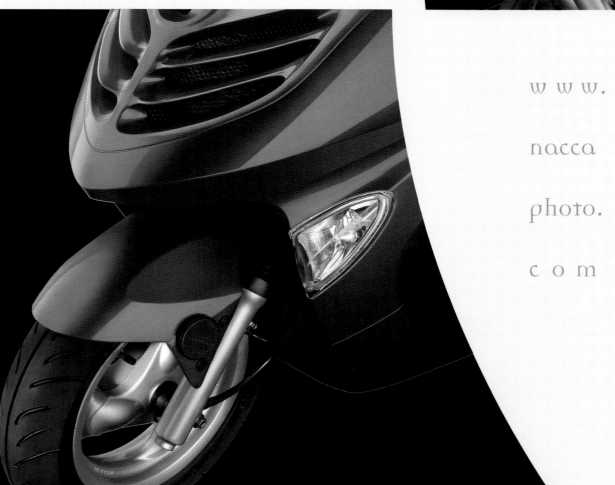

w w w.

nacca

photo.

c o m

Thomas Heinser

www.thomasheinser.com

415.495.0365

Elyse Connolly New York 212.255.0886

elyse@elyseconnolly.com

Derek Rothchild
323 463 2800
DerekRothchild.com
represented by Ann Koeffler
818 260 8980   annaetren@aol.co

ROTHCHILD

photography

nex

www.anthonynex.com
310 836 4357

eric myer photography | 310 589 5092 | www.ericmyer.com

eric myer photography | 310 589 5092 | www.ericmyer.com

VOLO PICTURES tristan davison and jeff mcneill www.volopictures.com

studio: 310.924.9301
represented by marsha pinkstaff 212.799.1500

1144

PASCAL DEMEESTER

maspeace

Norman Maslov Agent Internationale 415.641.4376 www.maslov.com

David Allan Brandt

Cristiana Ceppas

Michele Clement

Deborah Jones

maslov
.com

David Maisel

Mika Manninen

Peter Rodger

Stephen Austin Welch

maslove

Peter Rodger
peterrodger.com

David Allan Brandt

davidallanbrandt.com

Agent Norman Maslov 415.641.4376

Deborah Jones

deborahjonesstudio.com

David Maisel
davidmaisel.com

Agent Norman Maslov 415. 641. 4376

Michele Clement
studioclement.com

Stephen Austin Welch
saw-art.com

Cristiana Ceppas

ceppas.com

MIKA
●●●●●●●●

MASLOV 415.641 4376

west midwest

advertisers index

*Artist's Representative

advertisers index

*Artist's Representative

advertisers index

advertisers index

*Artist's Representative

advertisers index

advertisers index

*Artist's Representative

PUBLISHER
Alexis Scott

MANAGING EDITOR
Susan Haller

CREATIVE DIRECTOR
Ophelia Chong

ADVERTISING SALES DIRECTOR
Suzanne Semnacher

DIRECTOR OF PRODUCTION
Paul Semnacher

Creative
ART DIRECTOR
Anita Atencio

Advertising Sales
SALES REPRESENTATIVES
Linda Levy
Robert Pastore
Robert Saxon
Lori Watson

ADVERTISING ASSISTANT / NEW YORK
Francesca Meccariello

ADVERTISING ASSISTANT / CHICAGO
Janet Cain

Production
PRODUCTION MANAGER
Jamie Edwards

ON-PRESS PRODUCTION
Lynn D. Pile
Colin Yeung

PRODUCTION
Wendy Walz
Larry Gassan

Book Sales
Mark Williams

Accounting
CHIEF FINANCIAL OFFICER
Jere Clancy

ACCOUNTING ASSISTANT
Eduardo Chevez

FINANCIAL SERVICES
Richard Scott

CHAIRMAN OF THE BOARD
H.B. Scott

VICE-PRESIDENT
Ashley Butler

Workbook 27 Photography West • Midwest
BOOK DESIGN
More Milk Graphic Design
COVER
J. Shubin
END SHEETS
Stephen Chiang
COPY
Paul Gachot

photography 27

contents